PowerPhonics™

Giant Giraffes

Learning the Soft G Sound

Autumn Leigh

The Rosen Publishing Group's
PowerKids Press™
New York

Giraffes are giant animals.

Giant means very big.

Giraffes are very tall.

7

Giraffes have long necks.

Giraffes eat leaves from tall trees

Giraffes have long legs.

13

Giraffes can run fast.

Giraffes have horns.

Horns

Most giraffes have spots.

Giraffes are giant!

Word List

giant
giraffes

nstructional Guide

e to Instructors:

of the essential skills that enable a young child to read is the ability to ociate letter-sound symbols and blend these sounds to form words. Phonics ruction can teach children a system that will help them decode unfamiliar ds and, in turn, enhance their word-recognition skills. We offer a phonics-ed series of books that are easy to read and understand. Each book pairs ds and pictures that reinforce specific phonetic sounds in a logical sequence. ics are based on curriculum goals appropriate for early readers in the areas science, social studies, and health.

er/Sound: soft g – Have the child name words with initial consonant **j**. List words and have the child underline the initial **j** in each of them. Continue ilarly with initial consonant **hard g** words. Pronounce the following words d list them on a chalkboard or dry-erase board: *giraffe, giant, gentleman, neral, gerbil, gym*. Lead the child to conclude that the words in the third list ve the same beginning sound as the initial **j** words, but the same first letter as initial **hard g** words. Identify them as words beginning with the **soft g** sound.

onics Activities: Have the child tell whether they hear **soft g** at the beginning the end of the following words: *gerbil, change, giraffe, charge, giant, large, neral, strange, germ, cage, gentle, page, age, gym*. List the words in two lumns according to the placement of the **soft g** sound. Have the child derline the **soft g** in each word.

For two or more children. Create a board game with spaces leading along a path to the giraffe exhibit at the zoo. In the spaces, write words that begin with **soft g**. Prepare matching word cards and an illustrated chart of all the words used. Each word should appear several times on the game board as well as on matching cards. Players draw a word card and move a button marker to the next space in which the word occurs. Have the children refer to the chart if needed to read the word. Play continues until someone reaches the giraffes.

Make puzzles to review initial **soft g** words. For each puzzle, use a sheet of cardboard or construction paper. On it, mount a picture of an item that begins with **soft g**. Write its name two times, with **g** and **G**. Cut puzzles into four pieces, and have the child reassemble them.

Additional Resources:

• Denis-Huot, Christine, and Michel Denis-Huot. *The Giraffe: A Living Tower*. Watertown, MA: Charlesbridge Publishing, Inc., 1993.
• Ling, Mary. *Giraffe*. New York: DK Publishing, Inc., 1993.
• Wexo, John. *Giraffes*. Poway, CA: Wildlife Education, Limited, 1997.

Published in 2002 by The Rosen Publishing Group, Inc.
29 East 21st Street, New York, NY 10010

Book Design: Haley Wilson

Photo Credits: Cover © Johnny Johnson/Animals Animals; p. 3 © Telegraph
Colour Library/FPG International; p. 5 © Jeff Greenberg/Index Stock; p. 7 ©
John Giustina/FPG International; pp. 9, 11 © Ronn Maratea/International Stoc
p. 13 © Henry Ausloos/Animals Animals; p. 15 © David C. Fritts/Animals
Animals; p. 17 © Christian Michaels/FPG International; p. 18 © Bob Jacobso
International Stock; p. 19 © Howie Garber/Animals Animals; p. 21 © Roger D
La Harpe/Animals Animals.

Library of Congress Cataloging-in-Publication Data

Leigh, Autumn
   Giant giraffes : learning the soft G sound / Autumn Leigh.
      p. cm. — (Power phonics/phonics for the real world)
   Summary: To introduce the soft "g" sound, this book pairs words
   and pictures describing the physical characteristics of giraffes.
   ISBN 0-8239-5919-8 (lib. bdg.)
   ISBN 0-8239-8264-5 (pbk.)
   6 pack ISBN 0-8239-9232-2
   1. Giraffe—Juvenile literature. 2. English language—
   Consonants—Juvenile literature. [1. Giraffe   2. English
   language—Consonants]   I. Title. II. Series.
            2001
      599.638—dc21

Manufactured in the United States of America